# LONDON IN THE SNOW

In the series *Vintage Britain*

BOOK ONE
The East End in Colour
1960–1980

BOOK TWO
The Isle of Dogs

BOOK THREE
Dog Show 1961–1978

BOOK FOUR
Paradise Street

BOOK FIVE
The East End in Colour
1980–1990

BOOK SIX
London Underground
1970–1980

BOOK SEVEN
Hackney Archive

BOOK EIGHT
Butlin's Holiday Camp
1982

BOOK NINE
London 1977–1987

BOOK TEN
London in the Snow

# LONDON IN THE SNOW

HOXTON MINI PRESS

Trafalgar Square, 1947

# INTRODUCTION

Is there a better sensation than waking to discover it has snowed overnight? You can sense the stuff piled up outside even before leaving the warmth of the duvet. The slice of light leaking from the window that is, you're sure of it, a little brighter than it was yesterday. An unshakeable feeling that something has happened while you slept. An enchanting, muffled stillness.

Opening the curtains on one of these storybook-ish mornings turns you briefly into one of the Pevensie children, parting the fur coats at the back of an old wardrobe to find beyond it winter pure and true: flakes of frost swirling in the air, a powdered whiteness, the promise of an icy other-world.

In snow, everything looks softer, sleepier and more luminous – *'effet de neige'*, the Impressionists called it, and they devoted hours in the cold to realising it in paint. The sun glitters, blue-mauve shadows lengthen across the ground, the restless scissoring of tree branches is temporarily stilled. Corners, edges and intersections turn cushiony – each as round and plump as in a seven-year-old's painting. Traces of movement make accidental art.

Whether now, or 50, or 100 years ago, snow comes like a blessing, its thick fall a type of grace. It covers blights and eyesores (nature's version of vaseline on the lens, perhaps), it softens clangs and shouts. In its white wake, moods lift and camaraderie swells, while nostalgia – because this has a lot to do with nostalgia, doesn't it? – sugarcoats even the most boring activities.

In London, the effect is all the greater: the emptiness all the more pronounced, the silence all the more strange. And Londoners – even the oldest and most seasoned – never cease to be astonished by the world they have woken up to.

A few days in, of course, it's another matter: slush, treacherous pavements, and just plain cold. Bitter. Getting to or home from work, as many of these photographs show, becomes a kind of drawn-out Odyssean epic, complete with malevolent winds and the siren call of a quick half in a firelit pub to break up the journey. As for the dull weight of sodden wool, the throb of numb fingers and, if you're unlucky enough to be in school uniform, the blistering sting of exposed thigh flesh, I'm not sure the trauma will ever truly leave you.

But listen, that's an adult's view. To spend a while with the photographs on the following pages – with the gutsy boys testing the ice on a lake on Hampstead Heath, or the businessman in his plus fours pulling his daughter through Regent's Park on a toboggan, or the children pelting each other with snowballs in the playgrounds of Chiswick and Catford – is to be dunked to your middle in what I can only describe as snow-euphoria. Is there a word to describe that love of, or yearning for snow? If not, we should invent one. And a shout out, before I go, for the milkman pictured on New Year's Eve 1962, who, cigarette in mouth, is delivering his glass produce on a pair of razor-thin skis.

Lucy Davies
London, 2021

Fleet Street, 1965

Children walk to school in Peckham, 1938

Shoppers brave the snow in Kingston, 1939

Men push a car out of deep snow, circa 1960

Children play in a homemade toboggan in Ilford, 1958

Junction of Holborn and Gray's Inn Road, 1931

EDGWARE ROAD

Cyclists caught in a snowstorm, 1938

St Paul's Cathedral, 1965

Farringdon Street, 1951

Window cleaner on Clerkenwell Road, 1954

Office workers on their lunch break wait to cross
the road at High Holborn, 1966

Playground of Nightingale School in Hornsey, 1931

Shoppers queue up in Catford, 1948

Milkman out for deliveries on
New Year's Eve, 1962

Workers shovel snow in Piccadilly
Circus on New Year's Day, 1963

Trafalgar Square, 1963

Cyclist crosses the frozen River Thames
near Windsor Bridge, 1963

Street sweeper salts the ground in Trafalgar Square
on New Year's Eve, 1961

London Zoo, 1947

Hampstead Heath, circa 1960

Father and daughter in Regent's Park, 1929

Family toboggan on Hampstead Heath, 1945

Taxi and bus drive by Trafalgar Square, 1915

Models show off Mansfield's autumn collection on Great Titchfield Street, 1966

Crossing the Strand near Trafalgar Square, 1951

E LODGE
D 594

Schoolboys test the ice on a lake at Hampstead Heath, circa 1924

Policeman directs traffic, 1956

Catford School, 1946

Trafalgar Square, 1938

St James's Park, 1954

Hampstead Heath, 1939

Sledgers test out their new boards
after a blizzard, circa 1935

Horse Guards Parade, 1955

Arsenal players Ted Drake (*left*) and Eddie Hapgood train at Highbury, 1935

Charlton Athletic play Chelsea at The Valley stadium, 1947

Young athletes train at the University of London Athletic Ground
in Motspur Park, 1962

Guards play football at the Tower of London, 1929

Blackpool score their first goal against Chelsea
during a match at Stamford Bridge, 1947

Hampstead Heath, 1937

Ice skater encourages swans towards the open
water on Wimbledon Common, 1954

Schoolchildren walk past Tower Bridge, 1955

Student toboggans on Hampstead Heath, 1900

Alexandra Palace, 1935

Father and children toboggan on
Hampstead Heath, 1937

Hampstead Heath, 1955

Hampstead Heath, 1931

Footballer Geoff Hurst bounces a space hopper
across a snowy pitch, 1968

Streatham Common, 1938

New Year's Day at Hampstead Heath, 1962

Sheepdog carried by its owner, 1932

Milkman delivers to Streatham Grammar School
on New Year's Day, 1939

Boy carries loaves of bread, 1947

Feeding the ducks in St James's Park, 1942

Policeman sweeps snow outside Westminster, 1947

Terraced housing, circa 1960

Smithfield Market, 1947

City workers queue for a bus at London Bridge, 1962

Mother and daughter walk to school, 1969

Oxford Street, 1941

SWEARS
WELLS
The
UPPER PART
TO-LET

Staple Inn, 1952

Hyde Park, circa 1953

Couple skates past a worker sweeping snow, 1931

The wind carries off an umbrella, 1962

Hyde Park, circa 1953

Battersea Park, circa 1930

Frozen pond on Hampstead Heath, 1930

Skier is pulled along by a car in Earl's Court, 1962

Sisters stop for a smoke while skiing in Hyde Park, 1926

Child carries a Christmas tree home from
Spitalfields Market, 1946

Policeman walks along Embankment, 1933

Regent Street on New Year's Eve, 1961

Junction of Clerkenwell and Farringdon Roads
on New Year's Eve, 1962

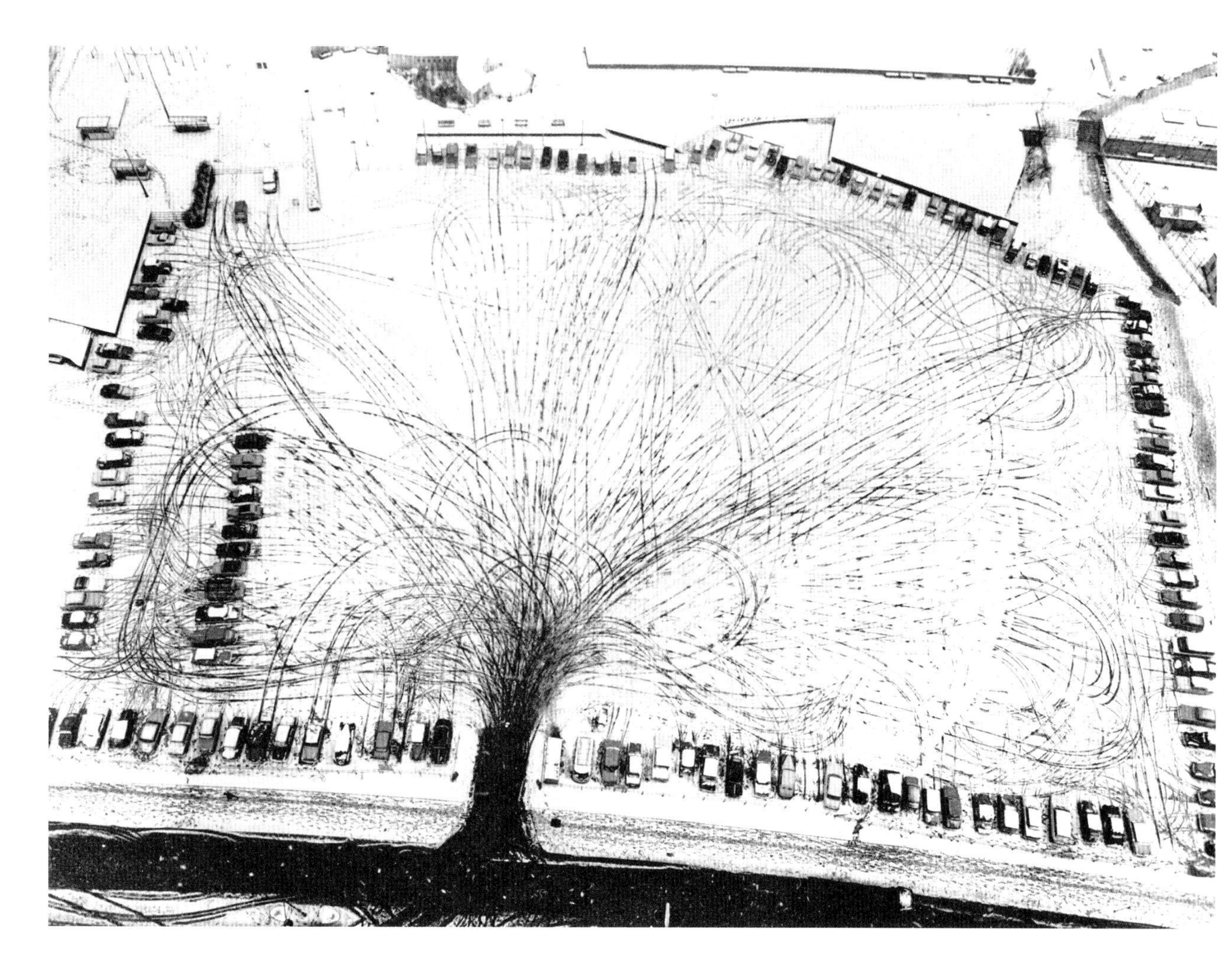

View from the 26th floor of the Shell Centre on the South Bank, 1963

Hyde Park, circa 1953

Regent's Park, circa 1960

Hampstead Heath, 1960

Bubble car, 1958

London Zoo's head keeper and Rusty the elephant
clear snow together, 1958

Bethnal Green, 1955

Wapping, 1955

Keeper counts the penguins during London Zoo's annual animal count, 1962

School playground in Chiswick, 1958

Cyclists collide, 1932

Hampstead Heath, 1935

Sioux Braves toboggan on Hampstead Heath, 1925

Actress Sally Ann Howes falls while
skiing on New Year's Day, 1950

Impromptu ice hockey game on the frozen lake
of Wimbledon Common, 1956

Rowers limber up for the Cambridge Boat Team practice race
between Chiswick and Putney, 1967

Hampstead Heath, 1955

NORTH END WAY NW3

Trafalgar Square, 1952

Deer graze in a London park, 1931

Milk float stops on Whitton High Street, circa 1960

Hampstead Heath on Christmas Eve, 1938

Buckingham Palace, 1982

Children sing Christmas carols in the street, 1960

The Trafalgar Square Christmas tree, 1962

Paddington Canal near Harrow Road, circa 1960

Sweeping snow in central London, circa 1930

St Paul's Cathedral from Ludgate Hill
on New Year's Day, 1957

Policeman directs traffic in Whitehall, 1938

Church Row in Hampstead, 1965

Grosvenor Square, 1968

Office worker walks through Walbrook
on New Year's Eve, 1962

Graveyard opposite St John's Church, circa 1960

Highgate Cemetery, 1982

Heath Street in Hampstead, circa 1960

Chevrah Shass Synagogue in Whitechapel, 1959

Dutch ship Lingestroom moored at Hay's Wharf, 1955

Westminster, circa 1960

Junction of Aldwych and the Strand, 1955

*London in the Snow*

First edition, published 2021 by Hoxton Mini Press, London


Design and sequence by Friederike Huber
Copy-editing by Florence Filose
Design support by Daniele Roa
Production by Anna De Pascale

A CIP catalogue record for this book is available from the British Library.


ISBN: 978-1-914314-11-7

Printed and bound by OZGraf, Poland

Hoxton Mini Press is an environmentally conscious publisher, committed to offsetting our carbon footprint. The offset for this book was purchased from Stand For Trees.

For every book you buy from our website, we plant a tree:
www.hoxtonminipress.com

Photography credits by page number:
4, 24, 25, 33, 52, 93, 105, 118, 119 © PA / PA Archive / PA Images; 7, 13, 26, 54, 74, 76, 77, 98, 111 © Keystone-France / Contributor; 8, 35, 53, 61, 58, 91, 127 © Hulton Archive / Stringer; 9, 62, 75, 78, 86 © Mirrorpix / Contributor; 10, 108 © Frederick Wilfred / Contributor; 11 © Ron Burton / Stringer; 14, 43, 57, 99 © Imagno / Contributor; 15, 96, 97 © Evening Standard / Stringer; 16, 39, 44, 92, 106 © Barratts / S&G Barratts / EMPICS Archive; 17, 87 © Colin O'Brien; 18 © Fred Mott / Stringer; 19, 49, 55, 59, 64, 82, 85, 100, 107, 116 © Fox Photos / Stringer; 21, 38 © Reg Speller / Stringer; 22, 71, 81 © Express / Stringer; 23 © Bob Haswell / Stringer; 27, 30, 36 © Hulton Deutsch / Contributor; 29, 68, 90, 120, 122 © John Gay / English Heritage.NMR / Mary Evans; 31 © Keystone / Stringer; 32, 69 © Topical Press Agency / Stringer; 37 © L. Blandford / Stringer; 41, 83 © Monty Fresco / Stringer; 42 © Stanley Sherman / Stringer; 45 © Popperfoto / Contributor; 47 © Barratts / S&G and Barratts / EMPICS Sport; 48, 102 © Sports and General / S&G and Barratts / EMPICS Sport; 50 © Central Press / Stringer; 51 © J. A. Hampton / Stringer; 60 © Terry Disney / Stringer; 63 © Mary Evans / Imagno; 65 © John Gay / Historic England / Mary Evans; 66 © Bill Brandt / Stringer; 67 © Bush / Stringer; 70 © Douglas Miller / Stringer; 73 © Daily Herald Archive / Contributor; 79 © Mary Evans / Hildi Reinhart Collection; 80 © George Rinhart / Contributor; 88 © Sport & General / S&G Barratts / EMPICS Archive; 89 © Staff / Zuma Press / PA Images; 94, 95, 113 © Roger Mayne Archive / Mary Evans Picture Library; 101 © Paul Popper / Popperfoto / Contributor; 103 © B. Thomas / S&G and Barratts / EMPICS Sport; 109 © TopFoto / PA Images; 110 © Michael Ward / Contributor; 112 © Kent Gavin / Stringer; 114 © Mary Evans Picture Library; 115 © George W. Hales / Stringer; 117, 123 © Heritage Images / Contributor; 121 © Historic England Archive / Mary Evans Picture Library; 124 © Harry Todd / Stringer; 125 © Mary Evans Picture Library / GERALD WILSON.